Fi

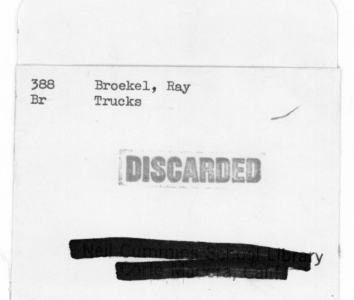

A New True Book

TRUCKS

By Ray Broekel

This "true book" was prepared
under the direction of
Illa Podendorf,
formerly with the Laboratory School,
University of Chicago

CHILDRENS PRESS, CHICAGO

Trucks often carry license plates
for more than one state.

PHOTO CREDITS

Marty Hansen—2, 7 (top), 9, 11 (top and bottom left), 18
(bottom left), 20, 25, 26, 35 (top), 41 (top), 42 (top and
middle)

Reinhard Brucker—Cover, 4 (top), 6 (2 photos), 7
(bottom), 14 (bottom), 16 (2 photos), 17, 18 (bottom
right), 22 (2 photos), 27, 28, 35 (bottom), 36, 42
(bottom), 44 (top)

©Ray Hillstrom—4 (bottom), 18 (top), 21, 38 (bottom)

Bill Thomas Photo—10, 11 (right), 12, 29, 30

Joseph A. Di Chello, Jr.—14 (top)

Tony Freeman—31

James P. Rowan—32 (bottom)

Jerry Hennen—41 (bottom), 44 (bottom)

Greyhound Lines, Inc: 1979 Tom Campbell—32 (top),
33

Root Resources—Weems, 38 (top)

James M. Mejuto—41 (middle)

Cover—Trucks on interstate

Library of Congress Cataloging in Publication Data

Broekel, Ray.
  Trucks.

  (A New true book)
  Includes index.
  Summary: Text and photographs describe truck
engines, fuel, bodies, tractor trailers, and the
specialized types of trucks used to haul or convey
specific merchandise.
  1. Trucks—Juvenile literature. [1. Trucks]
I. Title.
TL230.B68 1983   629.2′24   82-17907
ISBN 0-516-01688-1   AACR2

TABLE OF CONTENTS

Trucks can be used to move furniture.
Some trucks are used to sell food on street corners.

TRUCKS

Trucks are used in many ways.

Trucks are used to help people get the things they need to live and work.

Some trucks even make people smile.

Above: Tanker truck
Right: Dump truck

Trucks are motor vehicles. A vehicle is something that carries people or things.

Some trucks are small in size. Others are monsters.

They all run on wheels and have motors.

Cement mixer

This truck is pulling two trailers.

ENGINES AND FUEL

A motor, or engine, is a machine that uses energy.

In a truck engine fuel is burned.

The burning fuel produces energy. That energy makes the wheels move.

This truck is used to move horses from place to place. It burns diesel fuel.

Some trucks have engines that use gas as a fuel.

Other trucks have diesel engines. Those trucks run on diesel fuel.

CAB, BODY, AND FRAME

The cab is the part of
the truck in which the
driver sits.

The part in which goods
are hauled is the body.

The truck frame supports
the body and the cab.

Truck drivers sit in the cabs of their trucks.

11

Close-up of the cab, wheels, and frame

The frame holds such things as the motor and the wheels.

Another name for the frame is chassis. The chassis, or frame, is the running part of a truck.

Pickup trucks are small. They can be used to do many things.

TRUCK BODIES

There are many kinds of truck bodies. Each kind of body is made to do a different kind of work.

One kind of truck is the pickup. Most pickup bodies are uncovered. They have low sides. A pickup is used to haul light loads.

Above: This panel truck is used to deliver
dairy products.
Left: People often rent trucks when they have
to move things.

A panel truck has a
closed body. It does not
have a cab. The driver sits
on a seat inside the body.

Stores use panel trucks.
Goods sold in the stores
are delivered to customers
in panel trucks.

16

Platform truck

   A truck may have a
platform body. A platform
is a kind of floor.
   There may be a
framework around the
platform. The framework is
there to keep things from
falling off.

17

These vans all have bulkheads.

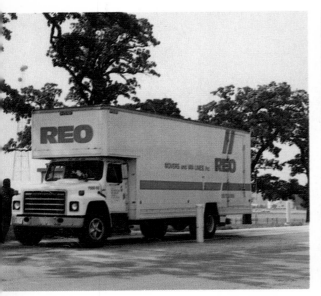

A van has a long closed body. It is used for carrying such things as chairs, tables, and TV sets.

Some vans have a part that reaches far out over the driver's seat. That part is called the bulkhead.

Goods can be carried in the bulkhead. Or there may be a bunk in the bulkhead. The driver can sleep in the bunk.

Dump truck

Dump trucks have heavy
bodies. They can carry
heavy loads.

The truck engines are
connected to pumps. The
pumps go up to tilt the
bodies.

Dump truck unloading from the rear

Some bodies tilt to the rear.

Some bodies tilt to the side.

The loads slide out when the bodies are tilted.

The pumps then lower the bodies.

Tankers carry liquid things.

Some trucks are tankers.
A tank body is a big
container.

A tank truck carries
liquid.

Some tankers carry
water.

Some tank trucks carry
liquid chemicals.

Some tank trucks haul
fuel oil. The fuel oil is
used to heat homes,
stores, and office buildings.

Some tankers are used to haul liquid food. Milk and chocolate are two kinds.

Liquid food tankers have special linings inside their tanks. The linings are made of glass or stainless steel. These linings are easy to keep clean.

Close-up of a tanker

Tankers are found at airports. They haul fuel to airplanes.

Other tank trucks haul gasoline to gas stations. The gas from them is stored in underground tanks.

Tow truck

Tow trucks are kept at some gas stations. Some car repair shops also have tow trucks.

Tow trucks are used to bring in cars that cannot run on their own.

TRACTOR TRAILERS

A truck can pull a much bigger load than it can carry.

A tractor trailer is a truck that hauls heavy loads.

A tractor trailer is made of two parts.

Cattle truck

The front part is called a tractor. It has a cab and frame, but no body.

The back part is a body called a trailer. It has big wheels only at the rear.

Tractor and its trailer

A driver slowly backs his tractor to the front end of a trailer. Two metal plates hook the two together.

Behind the cab on the tractor is a mounted round metal plate. That plate is called a fifth wheel.

At the front of the trailer is another round metal plate.

The trailer's metal plate fits onto the plate behind the cab.

The two plates turn
freely when the tractor
trailer turns a corner.

OTHER KINDS OF TRUCKS

Fire engines are special
kinds of trucks. They carry
fire fighters, ladders, and
hoses. Other tools to fight
fires are also carried in
the trucks.

31

Buses can be used to carry people on long or short trips.

Buses are special kinds
of trucks. Buses carry
many passengers.

Some kinds also carry
freight, such as baggage.
The baggage is stored in
the lower part of the
buses.

An automobile transport truck hauls cars from place to place. They carry the new cars made at a factory to car dealers.

The cars are driven onto ramps called loading ramps. Then the cars are locked into place. They cannot move about while being hauled.

Close-up of the bucket and support arm found on a repair truck

Special trucks are used to repair telephone lines or electrical lines.

These trucks have a bucket on them. The repair person travels up in the bucket.

Bulldozer loads a dump truck

Off-highway dump trucks can carry very heavy loads.

Off-highway trucks are big, heavy dump trucks. They are so big and heavy they would crack highways. So they are driven off the highways.

These trucks are used in construction work, such as building dams and new highways.

AT THE SUPERMARKET

Many kinds of delivery trucks bring food products to supermarkets. There are:
- bread trucks
- potato chip trucks
- soft drink trucks
- cold meat trucks
- frozen food trucks
- cookie trucks

People go to the supermarkets to buy these food products.

TRUCKS AROUND HOMES

You can see many kinds of trucks around homes.

Some take away things. Others bring things.

A garbage truck hauls away garbage.

A moving van may help a family move in or out.

Fuel trucks may bring coal or oil.

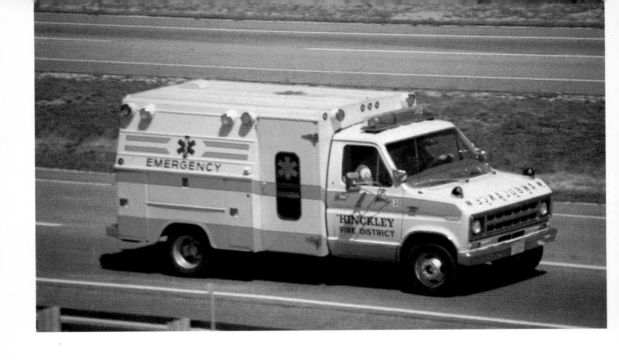

Mail trucks carry mail.

Special trucks bring sick people to the hospital. These trucks are called ambulances.

There are millions of trucks in the world. Night and day they are on the road working for people. Trucks are very important to our world.

WORDS YOU SHOULD KNOW

bulkhead(BUHLK • hed) — a part of a truck van that reaches out over the driver's seat.

cab(KAB) — the part of a truck in which the driver sits.

chassis(CHASS • ee) — the frame of a car or truck that supports the body and other parts.

chemical(KEM • ih • kil) — a substance that is made by or used in chemistry.

diesel-engine(DEE • zel EN • jin) — an engine that burns oil.

energy(EN • er • gee) — able to do work; power.

frame(FRAYME) — a form that holds other things; a support.

freight(FRATE) — goods that are carried in a vehicle; load; cargo.

fuel(FYOOL) — anything that is burned to give off heat or energy.

haul(HALL) — transport; carry.

monster(MON • stir) — a very large thing.

mounted(MOUN • ted) — to be set in place.

platform(PLAT • form) — a flat surface.

ramp(RAMP) — a sloping passage.

stainless(STAYN • less) — a type of metal that will not rust.

tractor(TRAK • ter) — the front part of a truck to which a trailer can be connected.

vehicle(VEE • hik • il) — anything used to move people or goods.

INDEX

About the Author

Ray Broekel is a full-time freelance writer who lives with his wife Peg, and a dog, Fergus, in Ipswich, Massachusetts. He has had twenty years of experience as a children's book editor and newspaper supervisor, and has taught many subjects in kindergarten through college levels. Dr. Broekel has had over 1,000 stories and articles published, and over 100 books. His first book was published in 1956 by Childrens Press.